WORKING MUM
… away with the fairies

Leanne Flower

Working Mum .. away with the fairies.

First Print Edition.

Copyright@ Eurika Training and Coaching Limited (2019)

All rights reserved. No part of this publication may be reproduced, stored in a retrieval system, or transmitted, in any form or by any means, without the prior written permission of the publisher.

ISBN: 978-1-5272-5168-7

Published by Eurika Training and Coaching Limited

Requests to publish work from this book should be sent to **leanne@leanneflower.co.uk**

Cover Design: Vanessa Myers

Printed by Amazon KDP Print

www.leanneflower.co.uk

DEDICATION

To my beloved husband, David Flower, thank you for always being there, supporting and encouraging me, for the 30 years we spent together. You will serve as my continuous reminder that life is a precious gift and one to be truly enjoyed. Rest in peace my love.

10% of all profits from this book will go to Cancer Research

To Lauren and Giorgia, for continuing to make my heart leap with love and joy. I'm so proud of the amazing women you have become.

To my inspirational working mum, Pauline Williams, for being my believing eyes and wind beneath my wing.

To all my wonderful clients, and fellow working mum friends, who have been the source of inspiration for this book.

TABLE OF CONTENTS

Ah, Good, You Found Us!	1
All Aboard! We're Going On A Guilt Trip ...	4
Want Something Doing? Ask A Working Mum!	9
Knock, knock ..Who's there?	12
Roll Up! Roll Up! The Juggler's In Town	17
So Tell Me What You Want!	20
LESSON 1: What Do You Want ?	25
Patience, Planning And Magic Goals.	33
LESSON 2: MAGIC Goals	38
Can't See The Woods For The Trees	44
LESSON 3: Solutions To Obstacles	50
How Do You Eat An Elephant?	53
LESSON 4: Milestone (mini MAGIC) Goals	57
No Time For Time Management	62
LESSON 5: The 7 Step Time Saver	69
Breakdown Before The Break-through? Get a LIFE!	78
LESSON 6: Get a LIFE	87
I Have Seen The Enemy And It Is... ME!	95
LESSON 7: Delegate & Say 'Yes' To Offers Of Help	100
Fill Your Own Cup	103
LESSON 8: Look After Yourself Before Others	111
PSST ... I Have A Secret	114
Have You Been Inspired?	125
Leanne Flower	126
Work With Me	127

AH, GOOD, YOU FOUND US!

Well hello there and welcome! How are you? No need to answer, we know...

You're feeling tired and tired of being tired.

You have feelings of guilt, guilt that you are not spending enough time with your family and friends.

And you feel that you're going to get 'found out' at work. You may look like you have everything under control but, like a swan, your serenity above the water hides your frantic paddling underneath.

You feel like you are juggling too many plates and the whole lot is about to come crashing down.

You have no 'me time' because any spare time you have you give it to those you love.

You're working so hard that you over-compensate at home by taking on too much of the household responsibility.

As fast as you earn money you spend it to make up for the lack of time you are spending with your loved ones.

And you're reluctant to accept offers of help because you want to show the world that you are in complete control.

You don't sleep well and have a never-ending to-do list...

Are we close? If not, this book may not be for you at this moment in time but please read on as we're pretty sure the lessons shared could help you or someone close to you in the future.

However, if the list above resonates wholly or in part with your story, then congratulations for reaching out and seeking help. It may comfort you to know you are not alone.

In this book you'll follow Laura's story and travel with her as she meets a variety of amazing working mums who share invaluable lessons on how to address some of the challenges you are facing right now.

We encourage you to read the book in the order it has been written but it's up to you as to when you complete the Exercises - complete them with Laura as you follow her on her journey, or do them at the end. All we ask is that you complete them, as your life will be positively transformed by doing so.

We trust you will love reading Laura's story as much as we've enjoyed sharing it with you and we're pretty sure that, after working through the Lessons, you'll have your own positive story to impart to other working mums.

Please grab a guiltless moment. Sit back, relax, and enjoy.

Your believing eyes

Hope and Flo
AKA The Working Mum's Fairies

ALL ABOARD! WE'RE GOING ON A GUILT TRIP ...

Laura hailed a cab at the train station, jumped in, announced her destination then slumped back and took a deep breath: the conference was over for another year. The last three months had been really intense in the build-up to the conference – there had been literature to prepare, people to organise, meetings to schedule. And the conference itself had been non-stop activity, filled with presentations, workshops, dinners with clients and meetings with the press.   And now? Laura sank back further at the thought of her post-event to do list, it seemed endless…

She arrived home, walked through the front door at 10pm, exhilarated yet exhausted! Her husband welcomed her, kissed her tenderly on the cheek, removed her suitcase and placed a glass of chilled wine in her hand then led her to the kitchen to talk about her trip and congratulate her on her achievements.

SCRATCH …. Don't be silly, that last bit didn't happen!!

HERE'S THE REPLAY

She arrived home, walked through the door at 10pm, exhilarated yet exhausted! With her suitcase in hand she struggled to open the door in the dark - how many times had she asked her husband to leave the outside light on to welcome her home?

Laura quietly opened the door but caught her shoe in the doormat and landed in a heap on the floor followed shortly by her bulging overnight case.

As she lifted herself up from the floor she caught a glimpse of her family snuggled up asleep on the sofa. Laura sighed with a mixture of heart-bursting love for her family and a dreadful guilt she felt at not being there to tuck her children into bed with a bedtime story.

She prised Amy, her youngest child, from the warm embrace of her father and sister, and carried her up to bed. Laura then returned for Jemma, her mini teenager - 9 going on 15! Laura's back groaned under the strain of Jemma's weight, "I'm too old for this" she reflected.

She tucked Jemma into bed, kissed her forehead, and stood in the doorway to listen to the peaceful sound of her children sleeping. Heavenly!

Laura's husband Pete passed her on the landing, bleary eyed and was clearly regretting the uncomfortable position he had assumed on the sofa. "Good trip?" he asked, not really caring for an answer. "I have to get up early in the morning, let's catch up tomorrow, night!"

"Night!" replied Laura, almost to herself.

Laura couldn't remember the last time she had gone to bed at 10pm. Lucky old Pete, she thought.

She wandered downstairs and gathered the school bags from the banister, poured herself a glass of wine and perched herself on a breakfast table stool. The wine tasted good.

The opening of the children's school bags was always done with trepidation. What events would the school spring upon unprepared parents this time? Laura was sure the school was on a mission to highlight inadequacies of mothers who had other commitments outside of the household. Was she being paranoid? Maybe.

She took another sip of wine and pulled out piles of crumpled paper. The first piece of paper offered the first challenge for an over committed parent: *Bring A Cake to School* for the charity fund raising day.

She looked at the paper again … The event was tomorrow! Oh come on, what about a bit more notice? She scanned the letter again. Dated over 10 days ago, ahhh…

Laura made a mental note to make sure the girls handed her letters each night when she came home from work.

The first thought that ran through her mind was, "Don't panic, you can buy a cake from the shop in the morning." Then an unwanted memory flashed into her mind… she'd tried to do that once before and it had resulted in Amy throwing a tantrum in the middle of the shop, announcing to anyone who would listen:

"I wish I had a normal mummy that didn't work. Suzy's mummy doesn't work and she bakes amazing cakes. Suzy's mummy loves her!"

Laura just couldn't go through that again!

She pulled out a cookbook and gathered ingredients to make fairy cakes knowing that even baking beautiful fairy cakes wouldn't console her daughter for not being at home to bake the cakes with her.

By 11.30 pm, the kitchen was filled with the aroma of freshly baked cakes. They looked wonderful – after she'd sliced the burnt bits off the bottom, removed the uneven tops, sliced them in two and placed them back on top of each cake with butter icing so they looked like butterfly wings.

She dusted each cake with icing sugar – magical! Laura marvelled at her creative flair and congratulated herself at being a Super Mummy, sooo talented!

She made her way out of the kitchen past the dog bowl and noticed that it was empty, poor thing! Laura put some fresh water in the bowl and added a little food. It was against the house rules to feed the dog so late at night, but she'd been away for a few days and wanted to spoil the dog – another pang of guilt got caught in Laura's throat as the dog looked up lovingly at her. Laura made a mental note to spend more time with the dog over the coming weeks.

*****

WANT SOMETHING DOING? ASK A WORKING MUM!

During the next hour Laura …

** Took the dog for a short walk
** Loaded the washing machine
** Set the coffee machine to percolate at 6am
** Opened the mail
** Paid outstanding bills online
** Checked the house was locked securely
** Finally made her way up the stairs to bed.

She quietly checked on the girls again – Laura always checked on them before she turned in, it was part of her wind-down routine and a comfort blanket. She slept better safe in the knowledge that her babies were safe and secure.

She noticed that Pete had left her nightie and toothbrush out so as not to disturb him when she eventually came to bed…

She crept into the bathroom and undertook the extensive task of getting ready for bed which included a rigorous skin care regime, teeth brushing, flossing, quick shower, body moisturiser, wrinkle reducing face and neck cream – damn getting older!

Right, nearly ready for bed.

She picked up her trusted pad and pen, she always carried around with her for moments like this, and quickly jotted down a list of, what turned out to be,15 items that needed to be done tomorrow.

Did she lock the front door? Better check just one last time…

Ahh…. the dryer had just finished. She quickly set about folding the warm clothes delighted that she had caught them just in time which meant that she would save herself half an hour of ironing later in the week. She switched off the kitchen light and made her final journey of the night up the stairs to bed. Pete was snoring loudly - great!

Making her way through the darkness to her side of the bed, Laura clambered in, pulled the duvet around her and laid her head on the plump pillow. At last! Ahh there's nothing like your own bed.

*****

KNOCK, KNOCK ..WHO'S THERE?

It was 3am and Laura was still wide-awake listening to Pete's snoring and vowing to herself to pick up some earplugs in the morning so she wouldn't have to go through such a painful night again.

4am. Still sleep did not find her. Oh come on… Thoughts flooded through Laura's head:

How can she be a better mum?

How can she achieve a work life balance?

Is there anyone out there who has achieved the perfect balance?

Who is the perfect working mum? Laura would love to meet her and discover the secret before the plates she was juggling (badly) came crashing down around her.

Something had to give but what and how?

A tear rolled down her cheek. What was that about? Exhaustion, guilt, loss of her own identity… maybe all those things.

She surprised herself when the silent tears turned into a loud sob. Help!

She crept downstairs quietly so as not to disturb Pete.

Laura caught a glimpse of herself in the hallway mirror. Her eyes were black through lack of sleep and the remains of the mascara (waterproof supposedly) that hadn't budged during her cleansing regime but was now rolling down her cheeks.

She didn't recognise herself! What had happened to the fun-loving girl who was going to change the world? "Look at you Laura, what a mess!"

"I have seen you looking better Laura, that's true," said a quiet but firm voice. "Come and sit down in the kitchen and tell us all about it."

Laura nearly jumped out of her skin. Who the heck said that?

"I'm sorry I startled you" said a beautiful looking young woman. "Don't be afraid, I'm Hope, your 'working mum fairy'".

"Oh my goodness I'm hallucinating," Laura grabbed the door handle to steady herself. "It must be the sleep deprivation, stress or that last glass of wine. Get a grip!"

"My goodness the poor woman is talking to herself, Hope," said a second voice. "You're right, she does need our help."

Laura span around and came face to face with a very haggard old lady "Argh!!!!" she screamed.

"Wow, I know I haven't got my make-up on but I don't look that bad, do I?"

Laura couldn't believe what was happening to her. She looked from side to side. On the left there was a beautiful young lady and, on the right, a haggard old lady. She covered her left eye then her right. Closed her eyes. Looked quickly from left to right again. Still there!!!

Laura made a mental note to book a holiday from work – perhaps she should see a doctor? Better not, they may lock her up and throw away the key!

The old woman looked at her again with concern on her face. "Here we go again Hope, another one in shock. I'll put the kettle on and make some nice strong sweet tea, bring her in when you're ready".

Hope smiled. "Will do Flo, give us a minute".

Hope held Laura's shoulders. "Laura, do you remember when you were a little girl and you used to leave gem sweeties at the back of your garden for the fairies?"

Laura thought back and smiled. "Yes, yes, I do."

"Well why did you believe in fairies then and not now?"

"I lost count of the number of times my parents told me they don't exist. When someone tells you something often enough you start to believe them. Besides I waited and waited by the fairy home and I never once saw a fairy. Anyway, you can't be a fairy you're too big."

"I am a fairy Laura. We only show ourselves though when you really need us and until now, Laura, you haven't needed us. But now you do so here I am, and I have brought my dear friend Flo with me, so we can bring some perspective to your current situation. Now, whether you believe that or not won't you at least just humour us and join us for a cup of tea?"

If I'm going mad, Laura thought, I might as well enjoy a nice cuppa. She laughed - slightly hysterically - and followed Hope into the kitchen.

The kitchen looked warm and cosy. The lights were dim and the smell of the home-made cakes still fragranced the air. Flo was leaning over the teapot.

Hope pulled out a stool and indicated for Laura to take a seat.

Flo placed a cup of tea in front of Laura.

Laura wrapped her hands around the cup, took a sip and spat it straight out "Blimey that's sweet! How many sugars did you put in it?" she gasped.

"Just sip it slowly dear, it's good for shock".

Flo pulled up a seat and sat beside Laura. Hope settled down on the other side.

*****

ROLL UP! ROLL UP! THE JUGGLER'S IN TOWN

Hope was the first to speak.

"We've been watching you for a while Laura. You should be so proud of everything you've achieved. A happy, loving family, great career, a wonderful home… but recently we've noticed that this doesn't seem to be enough for you. You seem to have lost the sparkle in your eyes that shone so bright when you were a child."

Laura shook her head and laughed sadly "Proud of what I have achieved, oh yeah… I'm *sooo* proud!

"At work, I have a to-do list at work that never ends and I feel like I'm always chasing my tail. I feel like my job is hanging by a very fine thread and that at any moment, I'll get 'found out' for being a fraud.

"As for my lovely home and happy loving family... I could rattle off millions of things that I want to do with my children but I don't seem to have the time. My husband and I are like ships that pass in the night, and as for my lovely home..." she sighed running her finger through a layer of dust on the shelf behind.

"I would love to have more time with my family and a nice clean home. I feel like a complete and utter failure. I'm juggling two jobs and I'm no juggler I can tell you!"

"Then stop juggling," Flo said calmly. "Why does your generation feel you all have to be Superwoman. I never felt the need to go out to work and leave my family with child care. Home-making was my job and I was very good at it. Why isn't that enough for you? It seems to me that you're making life difficult for yourself and there is a simple solution staring you in the face – give up your job!"

Laura looked at Flo, and put her head in her hands.

Hope rolled her eyes, "You're not helping the situation, Flo"

She put her hands around Laura's shoulders. "Times have changed Flo; we've talked about this" she mockingly scolded.

She turned to Laura, "I hear you loud and clear and we all know that you can't go on like this. Something needs to change. Are you prepared to go on a journey with us, so we can open your mind to a new way of approaching things?"

Laura laughed. "I'm sitting in my kitchen talking to fairies… so why not?"

"Close your eyes then dear," encouraged Flo.

Laura sat back in the chair, closed her eyes and started giggling. Hope and Flo exchanged looks, rolled their eyes and shouted "Ready!"

*****

SO TELL ME WHAT YOU WANT!

"Many people fail in life, not for lack of ability or brains or even courage, but simply because they have never organised their energies around a goal." American philanthropist Elbert Hubba

Laura's eyes were closed but she suddenly started to sense light around her and the scent of warm porridge wafted past. She opened her eyes. This wasn't her kitchen. Where on earth was she?

On the kitchen table there were half eaten bowls of porridge and beakers showing traces of orange juice. A moment later a smart woman dressed in a beautifully tailored suit entered the room calling behind her. "Come on, hurry up! You've got two minutes to get your shoes and coat on. Have you cleaned your teeth?"

She whirled round and, catching sight of Laura sitting at her kitchen table, took a small step back. "Oh no, not now, surely not! Hope, Flo .. really? You pick <u>now</u> to bring along a new cadet?"

Hope and Flo appeared.

Hope spoke. "Morning Jo! Sorry for just dropping in on you like this but Laura is really up against it at the moment; she's where you were a few years ago.

"Can we leave her with you for a couple of hours so she can see that she's not the only woman in the world trying to manage a stressful job and be a perfect housewife too."

Jo laughed. "Perfect housewife… okay I know what to do… leave her with me."

"Just Lesson 1 please. We'll cover the rest later," smiled Hope.

"Will do" replied Jo. "Kids come on, let's go go go…."

Hope and Flo disappeared.

Laura was flabbergasted. "I can't spend time with you I have to get back to my own children and get them ready for school."

"It doesn't work like that," Jo replied.

"The fairies have placed you in a parallel universe. They will teach you the lessons you need to learn and place you back where you came from before your family wake up."

Laura had already resigned herself to the fact that she was either dreaming or had lost her mind, so didn't even question the logic of the situation.

Jo's children appeared at the door, dressed and ready to go with lunchboxes and school bags in hand. Jo grabbed her coat, bag, and Laura, and the four of them shot out of the door.

Ten minutes later they arrived at the child minder's home. Jo pulled up, kissed her children before handing them over to the cheery childminder and then jumped back in the car.

Back on the road again, Laura clocked the speed.

"Why are we travelling so fast?" Laura asked

"We have 7.5 minutes to park the car and get on the train" replied Jo.

"What time is it?" asked Laura.

"6.45 am" replied Jo.

"Wow that's an early start for the children. Do they mind?"

"Hell yes!" laughed Jo." They moan and groan and they're grumpy but we've done this for 5 years so they're kind of used to it now."

"Anyway" she continued. "We'll talk more on the train. Come on – run!".

They parked the car and ran to the platform just as the train arrived. They made their way through the packed train, eventually finding a seat.

Laura turned to Jo. "The fairies asked you to teach me Lesson 1 - what is it?"

"Lesson 1 changed my life." Jo settled into her seat and started to reminisce. "Six years ago, I was feeling just like you: running around trying to be all things to all people, feeling like I was a failure and a fraud. I kept looking over my shoulder expecting someone to catch me out. My to-do list never seemed to get shorter – both at work and at home – and I hardly slept. I'm guessing this is where you're at now?"

Laura's face dropped "Yes, I sure am. But what did you do?"

"When I was at my lowest point Hope and Flo arrived and told me to stop. Just stop! Sit still and ask myself what I wanted from life. A simple enough question you might think but getting to the answer was far from simple.

"You see we spend all our time heads down, running around from pillar to post and not actually accomplishing anything that will make us truly happy. We're all so frantically busy we lose sight of what is important to us and that's when we start to lose our way.

"We forget that we have a choice, that we are in charge of our own lives and have the power to design the life we want. All we have to do is STOP, stand back, reflect, and then say what we want.

I sat down with Hope and Flo and they went through this exercise with me," said Jo, as she handed Laura a sheet of paper.

On the paper it read:

LESSON 1 : What Do You Want?

Imagine you walked past a cinema and you read the sign saying **"Now Showing – Your Perfect Life!"**

(Remember we are only looking at your perfect life from this point onwards, we're not interested in creating a perfect life for you when you were a child.)

Go into the cinema and purchase a ticket.

Imagine that, when you walked into the cinema, the film had already started and the scene showing was one where your life was just as you wanted it to be. It was a scene where work and home life were in perfect harmony, so much so that you felt lucky watching it.

Take a seat and look at the screen: what's happening in that scene?

Imagine describing this scene to a friend who missed the film. She likes a lot of detail so describe every little detail to her.

Please answer each of her questions below with as much detail as you can. REMEMBER: You are describing the scene from your perfect life:

- **What's your job?** Tell me about what you do, your responsibilities, where you work. What do you love about what you do? How do you spend your day and with who do you spend it (clients, colleagues, etc.)

- **How is your home life?** Describe your house, the vibe, what it looks like inside. How you feel when you are at home/in the garden?

- **How is your social life?** Tell me about your friends and how often you see them. What do you do with them? How do you feel when you are with them?

- **What's your emotional state like?** Explain the highs – what are you doing to feel really happy and content?

- **And what about your mental and spiritual state?** How does it feel to be in control and feel like you are growing as a person or owning your own place on this earth?

- **What's your financial status?** Let me know how you feel about being financially safe and secure. How do you know you are financially safe and secure? How do you behave now you know you have more than enough?

- **Finally how is your relationship?** Tell me about your perfect relationship. How do you feel when you are together? What do you do together? How do you treat each other, etc.

Laura threw herself into the exercise. She noticed she was smiling as it brought her such pleasure to imagine her perfect life.

She held the piece of paper in her hand and read the story of her perfect life over and over again to herself.

Jo was looking over Laura's shoulder. "Well done that sounds like a magical life. How do you feel?"

Laura looked up; she beamed: "I feel empowered!"

"Go on…" encouraged Jo.

"I just realised that I already have many elements of my perfect life. I've been so busy focusing on what I didn't have I didn't appreciate how many wonderful things I already have in my life. All I have to do now is make just a few tweaks and I can have my perfect life!"

"You see how powerful it is to just STOP and reflect on what you want from life?" said Jo.

"I know," replied Laura beaming. "Right, well where are Hope and Flo.... I'm ready to get back and start making changes ... I can't wait!"

"Hold on there!" Jo responded. "I felt exactly like you after I completed this exercise but remember that when you go back to your real life you will quickly slip back into your routine and forget this image of your ideal life."

"Is that why you're still manically busy?" Laura asked.

"Oh no," Jo replied. "Before I did this exercise I was in a dead-end job because I didn't feel I could take on a challenging role whilst I had young children. I felt frustrated as I was used to being in charge. I had turned into a 'Yes' person. I had lost both my identity and confidence.

"Believe it or not, I chose this life. It may seem frantic and manic but I thrive on it. I'm not saying this life is for everyone, but it works for me. It's important to make a mental note that what works for one mother doesn't work for another. Each of our ideal life scenes is unique."

Laura wrote at the top of her sheet of paper:

"You must not compare your life to others, or judge, or criticise the choices other mothers make ... we're all just doing our best to have a happy and fulfilling life."

Hope suddenly appeared in the carriage.

"Thanks Jo, wonderful work on Lesson 1. I'll take it from here"

Jo smiled. "No problem Hope. Now can you work your magic and get me to work on time?"

"Already done," Hope grinned and Jo disappeared.

Hope looked at Laura, "So what did you think of Lesson 1?"

"I loved it! It's so powerful. I want to start implementing changes now, but Jo said I'm not ready yet?"

Flo appeared beside her. "So... you want to return home immediately to start making changes?" Laura nodded excitedly.

"Hah these modern mothers!" scowled Flo. "They think they can take on the world. In my day we had patience. Unlike children today we waited until Christmas for a present. Children today are spoilt. They want everything now. I blame the mothers."

"Ohhh Flo, must you always be the voice of negativity? Times have changed. You're right though, information and goods are so accessible that people can have what they want much quicker than they could in the past but that's great when you're trying to change your life and make it better, isn't it?"

"I guess," answered Flo. "All I'm saying is, Rome wasn't built in a day and Laura must be realistic about what she can achieve."

"I agree," replied Hope, "and that's why we are going to teach her Lesson 2"

"What is Lesson 2" interjected Laura.

"You'll find out soon enough," replied Hope. "Close your eyes we're going to take you on another journey to meet someone very special."

SUMMARY OF LESSON 1

1. You are in charge and have choices.

2. Be grateful for what works in your life.

3. STOP and focus on what you want, not what you don't want.

4. Don't compare yourself to others, you are unique.

5. Don't judge others. We are all doing our best.

*****

PATIENCE, PLANNING AND MAGIC GOALS

"Life doesn't get better by chance it gets better by change" Jim Rohn

Laura opened her eyes. She was alone in a very modern meeting room with abstract art on the walls and floor to ceiling windows.

Through the glass she could see a well-groomed woman talking and laughing with a man. The man handed a pile of reports to the woman who then turned and headed towards the meeting room. Catching sight of Laura, she jumped a little then smiled and joined her in the meeting room. Closing the door behind her, the woman pulled the blinds.

"You startled me!" she said gently.

"Sorry," Laura replied. "The fairies placed me here"

"I thought as much, the room was empty just a moment ago when I left it. I'm Linda," said the woman as she held out her hand.

"Good to meet you," responded Laura, shaking her hand. "I'm Laura and I'm here to learn Lesson 2."

"Fantastic! I love Lesson 2," Linda grinned. "It made a huge difference to my life a few years ago. Can I assume you've already learnt how to take time out to reflect and document the specifics of your perfect life?"

"Yes indeed," said Laura. "And I can't wait to put it into practice but apparently I need to learn patience!"

"Absolutely. And that's where Lesson 2 comes in. Shall I share my story so you can see how patience and planning helped me?" asked Linda.

"Please!" replied Laura.

At that moment, two hot drinks and a plate of warm pastries appeared on the table. The women exchanged smiles. "Thank you fairies!"

Linda started to tell her story. A few years ago her life was chaotic: she was a single mum who worked very long hours; early mornings with late finishes. She hardly saw her children.

When she picked them up from the child-minder they were restless and demanding. They wanted her time and attention and didn't care what they had to do to get it. The children discovered very quickly that behaving badly brought lots of Linda's attention.

Every evening, when Linda returned home from work she felt tired and deflated, her head often hurt, she was hungry and she just wanted to sit quietly before starting back on that never ending to-do list. However, a hot evening meal to cook, and two children bickering and fighting for her attention, meant no precious quiet time.

She usually fell into bed exhausted and hated waking up the next morning as she knew the bad experience of 'getting on with life' would just keep repeating itself.

Linda was a PA and she'd just been transferred to a new manager who was very demanding with high standards. Linda made every effort to do a good job: her hours became longer as she checked and triple checked last-minute details of events and meetings to ensure they went according to plan. He would email day and night and Linda was always at his beck and call.

Despite her efforts the relationship between them was very strained, and she had just received a less than satisfactory appraisal which meant no much-needed pay rise that year.

She desperately needed a rise as her wages only just covered the family living expenses but there were no extra funds in the pot to take her family on holiday.

Linda felt the appraisal result was unjust - especially as she'd taken on the workload of her colleague who had recently been made redundant. She was doing the work of two people for no return – and she couldn't see how things could get better.

It was at that point that the fairies arrived and taught her Lesson 1.

Linda had also been very excited about the perfect life she had designed for herself and wanted to get working on it straight away but Flo (was she in fact more the voice of reason than negativity?) stepped in and taught her Lesson 2: The importance of creating MAGIC goals.

"Without writing MAGIC goals the journey to your perfect life could be very bumpy and long. MAGIC goals help you realise that there are quicker ways to do things – like choosing to travel by car rather than foot, or choosing a well-trodden path rather than going off road and hacking your way through brambles."

"I love the visualisation", laughed Laura. "I've definitely been hacking down brambles lately and getting scratched and tangled up," she added.

"We've all been there at some point in our lives," Linda reassured her. "Lesson 2 is like a travel guide beckoning you over and saying 'Come over here! Join us! The path's super easy and the view is great."

"I'd be like… no no not for me, that's too easy, I'll just keep hacking away thank you very much," giggled Laura.

"Ah, that was the old you. Have a go at Lesson 2 and let's get you fast tracked to achieving your perfect life"

Linda handed Laura a sheet of paper which read:

LESSON 2: MAGIC Goals

A perfect life doesn't happen by accident it takes time, preparation, consideration, and action. Read through the description of your perfect life and write a paragraph summarising what you want to achieve by when.

Then re-write each paragraph into a single sentence thus creating a MAGIC goal.

M – Measured
Ask yourself, 'How can I measure whether I've achieved my goal?' For example: 'I want more money' is not a measured goal as 'more' is too vague. Use specifics like "I will secure a pay rise of £3000 by Dec 20XX."

A – Attainable
For example, moving to Australia in three months will only be attainable if your visa application has been accepted and you have funds to get you there and live, etc. If you are just starting the visa application process you will need to extend your goal date to make it more attainable.

G – Greater Goal Orientated
Ensure that each goal you write will directly help you achieve your overall Perfect Life Goal.

Ask yourself if there is an easier way to achieve your greater goal; such as just ask for a pay rise! Achieving a Business Studies degree may not be necessary if you just want a pay rise, and may go against your greater goal to have more quality time with your family.

I – Inspiring
You are more likely to achieve your goals if they inspire you. You will be motivated to take action and with action, comes results. Once you've written your MAGIC goals ask yourself if they make you want to jump out of bed and do they make you smile when you read them?

C – Can Do Attitude
You must have a 'Can Do' approach to your goals. Relying on other people (or luck) to achieve your goals may result in you feeling disempowered and worse still, leave you short of achieving your Perfect Life. If you are not directly responsible for your goal, don't write it as a goal!

NB: It is said that individuals grossly over estimate what they can achieve in one year and grossly under estimate what they can achieve in five years – so go ahead and dream what you can have in five years then work back to what you feel you can achieve in one year.

"Got it?" asked Linda.

"I think so," mumbled Laura.

"Here, let me help you by sharing my goal," said Linda handing a second sheet of paper to Laura.

Linda's goal read as follows:

By XYZ date I will receive an outstanding result in my appraisal at work. I will have secured an annual pay rise of £3,000. My boss will treat me with respect and appreciate the work I do for him. I will work 9 – 6 and only work outside those hours if overtime is paid and as long as the extra work won't be detrimental to my children's wellbeing. My children and I will have quality time together at least three nights during the working week. My house will be clutter free and my garden will look like it is cared for. I will have deposited £200 per month into a holiday saving fund. I will cook fresh home cooked meals at least twice a week. I will take exercise of 30 minutes at least twice a week.

"Ah got it," said Laura.

"Sometimes it's easier to start with a five year goal and work back to writing a one year goal," Linda added.

Laura nodded her understanding and settled down to the task of writing her MAGIC goals.

A little while passed when Hope suddenly appeared out of thin air. "Hey ladies how was Lesson 2?"

"Very insightful," Laura exclaimed as she put down her pen and reflected on her goals.

"I bet you are going to say that you could achieve your goal quicker and easier than you thought possible?" replied Linda.

"That's right, how did you know?" asked Laura

"The same aha moment happened to me when I completed Lesson 2. Liberating isn't it?" Linda replied with a smile.

Laura looked at her MAGIC 1 year goals and delighted in the achievability of her Perfect Life.

"You see dearie, with patience and a little extra work it's easy to achieve goals without putting added pressure on yourself?" said Flo, tutting under her breath.

"I will definitely take time out to stop and write MAGIC goals when I feel my life is running away with me," blushed Laura.

"Ah time to learn Lesson 3 then. Once you master this lesson, life will never 'run away' with you again" said Flo smiling.

Hope turned to Linda, "Thank you for sharing Lesson 2. I am so pleased life is working out just as you planned"

"Nothing gives me greater pleasure than sharing secrets of success with another working mum," Linda turned to hug Laura.

"We'll leave you in peace Linda," said Hope. "Come on Laura, Flo is going to teach you Lesson 3."

"You know the drill Laura, eyes shut…" ordered Flo, and off they went.

SUMMARY OF LESSON 2

1. STOP and review your Life Goal

2. Create a five year plan to achieve your Goal

3. Break it down into one year MAGIC goals

4. Have patience and don't put too much pressure on yourself

*****

CAN'T SEE THE WOODS FOR THE TREES

Laura opened her eyes: she was surrounded by trees. She quickly realised she was in the middle of a wood and looked around for her next working mum teacher but noticed she was all alone.

"Flo where are you?" shouted Laura.

No reply.

"Okay the joke's over, where ARE you and where am I more to the point?" shouted Laura a little louder this time.

"I'm at the edge of the forest. Just follow the path and you will find your way out. Don't dither though – make sure you find your way out before nightfall as that's when these woods get dark and dangerous" said Flo, menacingly.

"Great! Thanks Flo! You may want to reflect on your teaching skills if you're taking Lesson 3," shouted Laura, shaking her head.

She looked around, taking in her surroundings. She was standing on a path that seemed to lead directly to the light beaming through the trees ahead of her.

"Oh this will be easy," Laura thought relaxing and set off on the trail exiting the forest.

However, several hours passed and Laura was tired, hungry, cold, and fed up. The path had disappeared some hours ago, the sun was starting to set and darkness beginning to creep in.

"Okay Flo, I give up. Come and teach me Lesson 3," she shouted. No reply.

"Come on Flo!!" Once again, silence.

"Arghhhhh! Seriously Flo!" yelled Laura, trying frantically to get back onto the path and find the light which could lead her out of the forest.

A few hours later the woods were cloaked in a blanket of darkness. Laura could hear the sound of the nocturnal forest waking, stretching and coming to life. She was scared. Thinking about the night before and her journey with the fairies, she realised that, despite doing Lessons 1 and 2, she was no closer to achieving her perfect life. In fact, she had a horrifying thought that when she got back to her 'normal life' she would feel exactly like she felt now – lost, scared, and overwhelmed. She sank to the ground with her head in her hands and quietly began to cry.

Seconds later there was a puff of smoke and Laura found herself safe and sound in a log cabin, wrapped in a blanket in front of a roaring fire.

Laura jumped as the whistle of a kettle announced it was time for tea.

"Have a nice cuppa," said Flo in a soothing voice.

She handed Laura a mug of hot tea. "Sorry dearie, I might have taken Lesson 3 a little too far. Still you'll laugh when I tell you why!" chuckled Flo.

"Hardly!" Laura rolled her eyes. "Go on then. What was I supposed to learn from that experience?"

"Well I used the woods as a metaphor for your current mental state. Remember that old saying 'You can't see the woods for the trees'? It means you're unable to understand a situation clearly because you are too involved in it.

"Let me talk you through this…

"When we met, you felt frustrated and overwhelmed. You had too much to do, felt you had too little time and you were consumed with guilt at not spending enough quality time with your family – especially your children."

Laura cradled her tea, nodding in agreement.

"We showed you two simple lessons to help you quickly determine what you want from life rather than wasting time and energy focusing on what you don't want. In a way we helped you get on the right path and showed you the light shining through the dark woods.

"If we'd placed you back into your reality after Lessons 1 and 2, in a few short months we'd have found you in a crumpled heap with your head in your hands sobbing – just as you were a moment ago in the woods. Nothing would have changed!

"Why? Because you have yet to learn Lesson 3: knowing where you want to go (your goal) is essential but you also need to make sure you have the right tool kit to help you reach your goal. By that I mean, you must be mentally ready to make a change, and then you need to plan your journey and gather the right tools and support before you set off.

"Think back to when I challenged you to find your way out to the woods. You immediately said 'This will be easy' as you knew where you wanted to go. Your goal was to follow the light as that would take you to the exit. But then you became surrounded by so many trees, that the path became obscured and you soon found yourself lost.

"Now if I had started you on your journey at the top of a mountain looking down into the woods you would have been able to see the clearing easily and could have prepared for the journey.

"You would then plan for your journey through the woods and set about gathering equipment and tools to help make your trip easy and comfortable.

"Perhaps you'd go into the woods with a map and a compass or maybe even a tour guide who knew the area well. You'd have the right clothing with you and be equipped with food, water and a tent, maybe you would have even done some survival training. You'd feel relaxed, safe in the knowledge that, because you were so prepared, you could survive overnight in the woods and eventually find your way out.

"All you'd then have to do then is breathe, place one foot in front of the other, and use your tool kit of items, training and contacts to get you to your target goal.

"Ahhh," said Laura, experiencing her light bulb moment. "You are so right Flo! I now realise that I am totally ill-equipped to make positive changes in my real life just yet! Although I still think your method of teaching was a bit harsh!" she added.

"Fear not dearie," Flo beamed, handing Laura a piece of paper. "Let's take some time out now to complete Lesson 3."

LESSON 3: Solutions To Obstacles

Reflect on your MAGIC goals and make a list of all the things that are currently preventing you from already achieving those goals. Then make a list of how you can change the situation.

For example:

MAGIC Goal 1: Finish work at 5.30 pm

Reasons why I am not currently finishing at 5.30 pm.

** 50 hours worth of work to do
** No assistant
** Management meetings arranged for 5pm
** Getting into office late so have to make up the time

Solutions
** Submit a proposal for additional support
** Recruit assistant or job share role
** Block out diary to avoid evening meetings
** Inform people of my boundaries re: evening meetings

** Share school run with husband and friends
** Request flexible working – work from home

Laura took a pen and frantically tackled what had prevented her from achieving her MAGIC goals.

In just 30 minutes she was done!

"Wow, Flo!" she exclaimed.

"I totally get the whole wood for the trees metaphor now. It's almost laughable that I thought I could go back to my old life and change things immediately."

"Don't be so hard on yourself dearie," said Flo surprisingly gently. "What might make you laugh now is how quickly you will achieve your MAGIC goals now that you have completed Lesson 3."

She reached over, rubbed Laura's shoulders, and gave her a little peck on the cheek.

"Ahhh look at you two getting along so well!" exclaimed Hope, appearing out of nowhere. "Everyone eventually flourishes under Flo's tough love."

"Ah get away with you," scolded Flo as she briskly started busying herself in the kitchen

Laura and Hope chuckled.

"Hope, that was such a valuable lesson. I'd love to say that I'm ready to go home and make changes but I'm hesitant as I now realise there is SO much more to learn. Sooo… I'm ready for the next lesson please."

"She finally gets it!" exclaimed Flo, clapping her hands happily! "Perhaps the youth of today are not as arrogant as I thought".

"Flo!" scolded Hope before turning back to Laura. "You've only got a few more lessons Laura and these won't take long at all. I'm going to personally take you through Lesson 4 and then I'll introduce you to some other amazing working mums so you leave this experience feeling truly inspired. Ready?"

SUMMARY OF LESSON 3

1. Appreciate that life will not change immediately.

2. Identify what is stopping you from having a perfect life.

3. Create solutions to those obstacles.

*****

HOW DO YOU EAT AN ELEPHANT?

"Okay! I'm ready for Lesson 4. Teach me everything I need to know!" exclaimed Laura to Hope.

"Have you ever heard the saying 'How do you eat an elephant? One chunk at a time," asked Hope.

"Yes and it makes me cringe to think of someone eating a poor elephant," winced Laura.

"Well it is just a saying, Laura," laughed Hope. "A metaphor for tackling something really big and overwhelming."

"Let me give you a really lovely example:

"Imagine you were faced with the challenge of securing an all-expenses paid luxury family holiday. Your tickets are printed out, with your names on them and packaged up beautifully in a box however that box is located at the top of a 100 storey high hotel.

"You are very excited at the prospect of your gift but then you learn that the hotel lift is out of order so you have to use the stairs... oh and you're not told the name of the hotel only the city in which it is located. How would you then feel?" asked Hope.

"I'd feel very excited about the gift but also frustrated and annoyed about how difficult it would be to find it," admitted Laura. "My initial thoughts would probably be 'Can I be bothered? Is it worth the hassle? And where on earth should I begin? Then I'd probably reach for a glass of wine and do nothing!" laughed Laura.

"You've hit the nail on the head!" nodded Hope. "Inertia is exactly what can happen when people are faced with something really challenging. Even if the person really wants to achieve the goal, the effort needed can often make them feel overwhelmed and result in them feeling like they can't achieve it. Then they self-sabotage by freezing and taking no action and so have no chance of reaching their goal."

"Blimey, that's deep," Laura frowned.

"It happens to everyone, it's not unusual. The trick is to have Lesson 4 up your sleeve so that you know what to do when you're faced with something that seems overwhelming.

"You simply have to break the goal down into easy bite-sized chunks and keep working your way through the chunks until you have completed the challenge.

"Let's now take one of your most challenging MAGIC goals and we can work out how to chunk it down into bite sized, easy to achieve pieces."

Laura read through her MAGIC goals and read her most challenging goal out loud.

"I will work 40 hours a week on a flexible basis so I can make cakes at home, attend school plays and be there if the children need me for after school activities."

"Great. Why did you choose that one as your 'elephant'?" enquired Hope.

"Because I currently work 60 - 70 hours a week either in the office or while I'm travelling. To be honest, as I was reading that out loud I immediately thought 'No way will I achieve that!" Laura laughed and then burst into tears.

"Hey Laura, it's okay," Hope put an arm around her gently. "Sometimes when our goals and ambitions seem so out of our reach we tend to give up and go back to leading an unfulfilling life. It's quite common. The fantastic thing is that you now have the golden opportunity to practice Lesson 4 on your most challenging goal, and in doing so you will be elated to learn that you can and will achieve it!"

"Really?" Laura raised an eyebrow.

"I promise," smiled Hope. "Let's work through this together and break it down into manageable chunks – Milestone MAGIC goals which can be likened to actions that you have to take to achieve your ultimate MAGIC goal."

Hope handed Laura a piece of paper entitled Lesson 4.

LESSON 4: Milestone (mini MAGIC) Goals

Review each of your MAGIC goals in turn and for each, answer these 4 simple questions. The answers will create your Milestone MAGIC goals:

What do you think has to happen first to make this goal take shape?

And what must happen then?

And what must happen then?

And what must happen then?

… repeat.

Laura started working through the questions. When she finished she read her answers out loud to Hope:

1. I will research the latest law on flexible working.
2. I will then prepare a business case for why I can be trusted to work flexibly.
3. I will also include a business case for a part time assistant.
4. I will turn the spare bedroom into an office.
5. I will educate my colleagues on my new working times, procedures, and boundaries (e.g. only answer emails between certain hours).
6. I will secure additional help at home for tasks such as cleaning and ironing so that I can give my children my full attention when they need me.
7. I will educate my children and husband of my work boundaries so that we can all benefit from my new working arrangement.

"That's fantastic Laura, well done!" exclaimed Hope.

"We'll see," said Laura. "What if my boss doesn't agree with this idea?"

"Well… if he doesn't then at least you've tried to improve. You then have other options: keep trying to find a solution, find another job that is more flexible or even start up on your own.

"The good news is, you don't need to worry about the 'What ifs' at this stage. All you need to do is write down the milestone MAGIC goals and start working towards achieving them.

"If they don't work out as you had planned then simply write another milestone MAGIC goal and keep on taking action. That's all you can do. Write a goal, take action, reflect or rejoice, or repeat."

"You're right! What's the worst that can happen?" announced Laura.

"The worse that can happen is that you continue to ignore Lessons 1 to 4 and go back to how you were. Nothing ventured, nothing gained, eh?" said Hope with a big smile on her face.

"Indeed! In for a penny in for a pound" laughed Laura.

"What the heck does that mean?" asked Hope.

"I have no idea," laughed Laura.

"Right! Down to business!" said Hope in her best teacher's voice. "Apply Lesson 4 to all of your MAGIC goals and then we can stop for a bite to eat to celebrate."

Laura picked up her pen and started to scribble milestone MAGIC goals.

It took her just 30 minutes – it was far quicker than she had imagined.

"I know I can achieve these MAGIC goals – they seem so manageable!" announced Laura.

"That's the point of the exercise," laughed Hope. "But remember, it is vitally important that you make a list of actions that you need to take in order to achieve your milestone MAGIC goals. Date the actions in order of priority. Then take the top five to nine priority actions / milestone MAGIC goals and put the rest on a separate list.

"Humans can only manage five to nine items on their to-do list at any one time. Anymore and they will start to feel overwhelmed and inertia will set in. Promise me you will do this last critical step?" urged Hope.

"Of course" agreed Laura, "It makes perfect sense" then she set about writing her actions.

Just as Laura completed her actions her tummy began to rumble: "Must be time for a treat," she grinned at Hope.

"Did someone mention food," boomed Flo appearing out of thin air.

"Time for tea and cake," laughed Hope. "I'll put the kettle on.

After tea and cake Hope turned to Laura and announced: "Now we've taken care of your rumbling tummy we need to introduce you to an incredible working mum who can teach you how to make the most of your time,"

"I'm ready" replied Laura, closing her eyes.

SUMMARY OF LESSON 4

1. An ambitious goal can be debilitating.

2. Break MAGIC goals down into smaller milestone MAGIC goals.

3. Make a plan of how you will tackle each milestone MAGIC goal.

4. Work on no more than nine Milestone MAGIC goals at any one time.

5. Only have a Plan A. Plan Bs detract from Plan A .

*****

NO TIME FOR TIME MANAGEMENT

When Laura opened her eyes, she found herself in a park.

Hope and Flo were nowhere to be seen but several children were looking up to the sky. Laura wondered if they believed in fairies and felt their existence.

She looked around at the smiling faces of children playing on swings and slides and chasing each other around trees and wished for one moment to be a child again with no responsibilities, just living in the moment.

"Penny for your thoughts?" said a woman holding a toddler's hand.

Laura shook herself out of her daydream and smiled at her inquisitor.

"I was miles away. I was just thinking how great it would be to be young again with no responsibilities. No dinners to prepare, no bills to pay, no boss to answer to, no husband to run after, no errands, no guilt that you haven't seen your mother or called your grandmother or missed your friend's birthday," Laura rambled.

"You need a magic fairy to help you," announced the toddler. "My mummy has two!"

"It's funny you should say that," laughed Laura kneeling down to talk to the toddler. Then realising what the toddler had said and noticing that she was in a park dressed in winterwear, she looked up into the twinkling eyes of the child's mother.

"I guess I'm here to teach you Lesson 5," grinned the mother. "I'm Alison and this is Eva."

The toddler let go of her mother's hand and ran to join her friends in the playground.

"There's a bench over there with our name of it," said Alison gesturing for Laura to sit down.

"How did you know that I am here to learn Lesson 5?" asked Laura

"Hope always sends working mums to me for Lesson 5. It's my forte."

"I'm intrigued. What's Lesson 5?" enquired Laura.

"It's time management!" Alison smiled.

"Time management! I don't have time for time management," replied Laura. The women laughed as Laura realised what she had said.

"Ok, ok... consider me your willing student. Please teach me what I need to know," conceded Laura while secretly wondering what Alison could teach her about time management as she clearly only worked part time or didn't work at all since she was in the park with her toddler on a weekday.

"I bet you've assumed that I work part time or not at all?" asked Alison.

Laura went bright red.

"And no, the fairies haven't given me the gift of mind reading!" laughed Alison

Laura looked startled and blushed even deeper.

"It's okay," Alison chuckled. "I've delivered this lesson so many times I know exactly what people think. Let me tell you my story."

"My life aim is to have a good work life balance. My career must fit around my family and not the other way around. That's my personal goal. I have a vision board of it. It is included in my MAGIC goals and every decision I make revolves around this goal.

"However, it hasn't always been this way. I've only been clear about this since the fairies visited me and taught me Lessons 1 to 4. Before then I got caught up in the cycle of working hard and neglecting my family, or doing less work and feeling like I had no identity. When I achieved success in either work or home life the other would suffer. I was in a continuous state of stress carrying around a big bag of guilt and unhappiness by trying to please everyone apart from myself.

"After documenting my goals and working out what I really wanted from my life, I realised that I wanted a demanding career that fitted around my family and so I started to design that life for myself.

"I now work 50-60 hours a week, travel all over the world on business and have a great relationship with my children. My poor husband doesn't seem to see much of me but we've come to an agreement that this works in the short term and we'll review that before it becomes uncomfortable."

"Incredible," replied Laura "But how do you work 50-60 hours and travel when you have a toddler?"

"And a 6 year old in school. Flexible hours – that's the key for me."

"I work for a great company who respect the work that I do and know that I have their best intention at heart. They trust me to meet my objectives and know that I always exceed their expectations," explained Alison.

"We made an agreement which suits us both. I have contracted hours and I work them when it suits them and me. This means that I can take my children to school and pick them up. I can go to school concerts. I'm there to tuck them into bed most nights and I'm there for most of the school holidays."

"My family and I also made a vision board together so they know that I am working to achieve things on our vision board; like a holiday or new clothes, or trips to the Zoo or bunk beds, etc," explained Alison. "My children get excited when I go away on business because they know they are one step closer to achieving their goal. There is no guilt because I know in my heart of heart that what I am doing at any moment in time is right for me, my employer and my family."

"You sound so content. It must be wonderful to have a boss like that. I don't think that my employer would be so accommodating," said Laura.

"Remember what Hope said about choices?" asked Alison

Laura nodded.

"Really?" questioned Alison

"Yes!" replied Laura defensively

"Well then you will know that you have a choice. You can decide whether you want to continue working for that employer in the same old way or find a new way of working. You could find a new employer who matched your values, or even set up your own company. You have a choice Laura, the hard bit is deciding what you want and working out how to achieve it," Alison smiled reassuringly.

"So true…" Laura said quietly.

"You already know what you want to achieve and how you are going to achieve it. Just stick to your plan. And remember – don't compare yourself to others!"

"The stumbling block for you now will be how do you include your milestone MAGIC goals actions into your already busy schedule. Am I right?" asked Alison

Laura nodded.

"Let me share with you the exercise the fairies did with me some time ago. I revisit it regularly."

LESSON 5: The 7 Step Time Saver

This lesson promises to give you back the gift of time.

Albert Einstein's definition of insanity is doing the same thing over and over again and expecting a different result.

If you want your life to change for the better now is the time to start doing things differently.

By working through this exercise, you'll learn where you are wasting time and where you are doing unnecessary tasks that could be delegated to someone else or deleted entirely.

Grab a large piece of paper and green, blue, pink, and black coloured pens, then work through the following exercise.

Step 1
Think about how you spend your day and itemise each activity in detail

1. Itemise every single thing you do as part of your job?

2. Itemise every single thing you do in your personal life in your role as
- Mother
- Wife or partner
- Daughter
- Sister
- Friend
- Neighbour

Here are a few things to get you started:
Washing clothes, ironing, loading and unloading dishwasher, creating a shopping list, shopping, unpacking the food, cooking, lunch boxes, home work, storytime, school run, booking holidays, going on holiday, buying cards and presents, Christmas (shopping, preparation, etc), bedtime routine, nights out, watching TV, relaxing, exercise, emails, meetings (staff, clients, prospects), filing, accounts and book-keeping, paying bills, travel arrangements, travelling time, appraisals, HR, IT, business planning, sales, marketing, networking, browsing the web, social media, flyers, e-campaigns, reading and research, training, diary management, client work, sleeping.

Step 2
Calculate how much time you spend on each activity per week on average.

NB: There are 24 hours in a day, 365 days in a year so you have 8760 hours available per year. It is recommended that you have at least 7/8 hours sleep a night so that's 2738 (on average) per year leaving you 6022 waking hours.

How many hours did you calculate?

Was it greater than 6022? If it was great! You've answered honestly and you're a normal working mum who feels she has too much to do and has too little time to do it! This prompts the feeling that you are underachieving when in fact you are over achieving in all areas, you just have unreal expectations of what can be achieved by when.

NB: If your hours weren't greater than 6022 then think again and come back to the task tomorrow – you're bound to have other tasks to add to your list that you'd forgotten you perform!

NB: During the next steps you can place more than one colour by each item

Step 3
Take a green pen and place a circle next to each item that contributes to your MAGIC goals.

Step 4
Take a blue pen and place an X next to each item that doesn't contribute directly to your MAGIC goals.

Step 5
Take a pink pen and draw a love heart next to each item you love to perform.

Step 6
Take a black pen and place an X next to each item that you hate to perform.

Step 7
Insights and actions

- **Green circle and pink heart**

Keep doing this – it contributes to your MAGIC goals and you love doing it!

- **Green circle and black x**

Delegate this as quickly as you can or try to find a way to make this an enjoyable experience, knowing that by doing that activity you are directly contributing to your MAGIC goals

Calculate how much time you will save if you delegated this activity [box]

- **Blue circle and pink heart**

You may love to do this activity but it isn't contributing to your MAGIC goal and it's getting in the way of you getting what you really want in life.

Ask yourself:
Why are you doing that activity?
Does it need to be done at all?
Can someone else do it so you can concentrate on Green Circle Activities?
What could you be doing if you didn't do this item i.e. opportunity cost

Delegate or delete this activity or, if you really can't let it go, do it only if you have time after your Green circle activities. Consider slotting it in between your Green circle activities to revitalise you when you need more energy.

Calculate how much time you will save if you stopped doing this activity [box]

- **Blue circle and black x**

They don't contribute to your goals and you don't like doing them so delete or delegate.

Calculate how much time you will save if you stopped doing this activity [box]

NB: It's perfectly normal to think that you can't delegate or delete activities, or it's impossible to do so, but try switching your thinking from **"I can't ..."** to asking, **"How can I ....?"** The answers and solutions will find you if you are motivated enough to pursue your new perfect life goal.

Finally add up the hours saved boxes and write the total here in big bold numbers: [box]

You have that many hours now to dedicate to your Milestone MAGIC actions that will directly help you achieve your MAGIC goals.

Congratulations and welcome to the path of achieving what you want in life!

"When you're ready…" said Alison, handing paper, coloured pens, and some Post-It notes.

Laura threw herself into the exercise. She found that the list of tasks came in waves. At first they came gushing out and then, just as she thought she had nothing else to add, she added another wave of actions. This process carried on for half an hour and then, once she was sure no more tasks were coming, she took the coloured pens and started working out what she should do, delegate and delete.

When she finished, she looked at the colourful board in front of her and turned to Alison.

"Wow! That was insightful, I feel very proud of myself and what I actually accomplish in a day."

Alison broke into song *"I am SuperWoman, Yes I am, Yes she is …"*

"Alicia Keys!" Alison and Laura shouted and laughed in unison.

"Mummy! STOP!! You're embarrassing me," scolded Eva who was playing in the sandpit with another little girl.

"That's us told," said Alison laughing with Laura.

"In my day if you were laughing you weren't learning ... we're going to have to spend more time with Laura to go through Lesson 5," tutted Flo.

Laura and Alison looked at each other and burst into laughter again.

"Oh Flo, please don't worry I have well and truly grasped Lesson 5. It's the most interesting, insightful and life changing exercise of all. I truly understand that I have been ploughing my time and energy into areas that are not fully serving me and I fully intend to stop doing that – immediately" said Laura with conviction.

"Ahh that's the Laura I know and love. You have that get up and go look in your eyes. I have seen that look before when you were determined to ride your bike without stabilisers. You were scared, excited and determined all at the same time and then you were exhilarated when you took off down the street shouting "Look at me! I can do it!" remembered Hope.

"I remember," smiled Laura nostalgically. "And you're absolutely right, that's exactly how I feel now. I feel that I have the insight, knowledge, and motivation to go out there and start fulfilling my dreams"

Hope turned to Alison, "Alison you've done it again! Another satisfied customer".

"It's my absolute pleasure," replied Alison.

"Nothing brings me more joy than sharing lessons I've learnt with others, especially when you know they are going to implement what they've learnt and will change their life for the better because of that knowledge and action."

"Absolutely," shouted Flo, Hope and Laura in unison and they all fell about laughing.

"Okay that's enough of that," boomed Flo suddenly. "Let's get Laura learning Lesson 6 before we all forget why we're here!"

"You know the drill Laura," added Flo.

Laura mouthed thank you and goodbye to Alison and dutifully shut her eyes.

SUMMARY OF LESSON 5

1. Be conscious of every activity you perform.

2. Pay attention to activity that is detracting you from achieving your MAGIC goals.

3. Learn how to delegate items so you can focus on the important stuff.

4. Let go of activities that are not serving you.

5. Keep doing things that contribute to your perfect life goal

*****

BREAKDOWN BEFORE THE BREAK-THROUGH? GET A LIFE!

When Laura opened her eyes she was sitting on a tall stool in a chic cocktail bar. Relaxing jazz and blues music was playing in the background and there was a gentle hum of chatter. Laura caught sight of herself in the mirror and saw that she was 'dressed up' – wearing a knee-length skirt that draped exquisitely, perfectly chosen accessories and a cashmere throw to keep out the evening chill. It was a good look.

"I agree, you look lovely," said a voice. Laura turned around startled and embarrassed that she'd been caught looking at herself in the mirror.

"So sorry! I didn't mean to startle you," said an elegant looking woman. "I'm Fiona. Have you come to learn Lesson 6?"

Laura chuckled. "Hi Fiona, yes I have. I won't even ask how you knew that. I'm starting to get used to how this works now. I'm Laura."

"I know," replied Fiona laughing and wrapped her arm around Laura's shoulder and led her to a table for two.

Laura sat down and quickly scanned Fiona's appearance. She was in her early forties, slim and elegant and dressed in beautiful, feminine tailoring with shoes to die for!

"I've taken the liberty of ordering a drink and food for you, hope that's okay?" Fiona raised an eyebrow.

Laura nodded with delight, thrilled at not having to make a decision about her menu choices (although she secretly hoped she'd like Fiona's choice).

"Don't worry, Hope helped me place your order, she knows you very well," Fiona smiled.

"Okay, to business. Tell me briefly about the insights you have learnt so far," asked Fiona.

Laura talked excitedly about Lessons 1 to 5

1. You can have what you want you just have to specify what that looks like, feels like, and sounds like.

2. You have to make MAGIC goals so you know what you want and when you are going to get it.

3. MAGIC goals need to be broken down to make them manageable.

4. You must take considered action, knowing that by taking action you will get closer to achieving your goals.

5. You have to let go of the old in order to reach for the new which means you have to delegate or delete some tasks and focus on tasks that contribute directly to your goal.

"Brilliant" exclaimed Fiona. "That's exactly right. You seem buzzing with energy and I bet you can't wait to get started on Lesson 6?"

Laura nodded. "To be honest, I'm getting a little frustrated: I want to get on and start making changes for the better now!"

"Ahhh, but that's exactly why you need to learn Lesson 6 because without it you're going to quickly hit your 'wall', " explained Fiona.

"My wall?" Laura looked confused.

"Yes," replied Fiona. "Without knowing it you've already changed. Not physically, but mentally. You have a different outlook, you've been handed the gift of insight and knowledge that a better way exists. You have energy, passion, enthusiasm... with all that comes action and changes and some people don't like that.

"They will start to 'get in your way'. They're not doing it intentionally, they usually acting out of fear – fear that you'll change so much that you'll leave them behind. And so they'll do what they can to keep you where you are and get life back to normal."

"But surely if these are people who know, love and trust me they will support and encourage me?" Laura was confused.

"Eventually they will but not at first. You have to show them that you are serious about making changes and help them see that change is good and will result in better things for all of you.

"Your language and actions all have to align with your MAGIC goals; your intention. As soon as you start acting out of alignment people will jump on it and convince you that the 'old way of doing things' is the 'best way of doing things,'" added Fiona.

"When you go back you have to have unshakable conviction in your actions and your behaviour and stick to your resolution that you are doing this for the good of everyone – especially you – because, as we all know, if we are happy then those around us are happy," stated Fiona.

"Wow! That's insightful," nodded Laura. "It didn't cross my mind that those around me wouldn't support me from the start."

Laura looked across the table at Fiona, "You look really together, how do you do it?"

"If only you knew what I've been through!" Fiona laughed. "I own my own business and my biggest obstacle was my clients. My goal was to organise my work to fit around my children and school hours. I was absolutely determined that I could earn the same, if not more money, by working smarter rather than harder.

"Following the fairies' advice, I noted every activity into my diary. Work time, home time, toilet breaks – I'm not even joking – you name it I allocated a time to it. I returned home after Lesson 5 incredibly passionate about my MAGIC goals and was utterly determined to make my goals happen.

"But by the end of the first month I was completely disillusioned and deflated because, not only did I find that I was back in the same boat but, the pressure on my time was becoming increasingly tight. I felt worse than I did when the fairies found me before Lesson 1".

Laura was listening intently, "Please tell me it all turned out okay in the end…"

"Oh Laura," smiled Fiona. "As much as I would love to cut to the chase and reassure you, you must hear about the whole journey to help you cope with the changes in store for you too."

"I'm listening…" replied Laura.

Fiona continued: "There I was head in hands sobbing again, mascara running down my cheeks, when the fairies arrived and gave me another heap of great advice. They told me that before the breakthrough comes the breakdown.

"It's your ego stepping up and trying to keep you playing small. Your ego doesn't like you to change because it is comfortable with you playing small – small is safe. Your ego is scared you'll outgrow it and leave your old self and old ways behind which would ultimately lead to leaving it, the ego, behind. And so it will do all it can to keep you from changing and growing.

"Here's how this manifested itself in my life:

"My main client called me at all hours of the day and night and showed no respect for my commitments and working hours. This put extra pressure on my family and 'me' time. I felt resentful and guilty that I wasn't spending quality time with my children.

"My children then became ill and I had to look after them in the day which meant I had to work late into the night or start really early in the morning, which was exhausting. I lacked concentration and this resulted in small mistakes appearing in my work. I felt like I wasn't being a good mother or a good businesswoman.

"My childminder then resigned which meant I had to find more hours in the day so I could look after the children and undertake the task of finding a new childminder. The children became unsettled and I felt guilty that I was leaving them with yet another childminder. You can see how all this pressure could easily cause a working mum to question why she is bothering to work?"

Laura nodded in agreement as Fiona continued.

"You question your motives for putting yourself and your family through all this and feel like you are the most selfish person on the planet. The pressure and the guilt is just too overwhelming and presents itself as a 'mini-breakdown.

"The fairies told me that when you get to that point you should celebrate because just around the corner is your breakthrough. When you feel at your lowest, sit back and ask yourself "What am I being called to learn?" And get excited about what's around the corner.

"They told me that blocks present themselves to show us how badly we want something. And often blocks can present themselves as people."

"Why is that?" asked Laura.

"Well once you set your MAGIC goals for your perfect life you're acting at a higher level of consciousness. Things that didn't bother you much before suddenly become magnified as you become very aware of what you don't want in your life. When they become fully magnified this is your opportunity to find a way to change the situation by offering a win win solution."

Fiona reached into her handbag and pulled out a sheet of paper and placed it on the table in front of Laura.

"Do you remember during Lesson 3 that you were taught to carry around a tool kit to help you with challenging situations?" Fiona asked.

"Yes," replied Laura, recalling Flo's harsh methods of teaching her that lesson in the woods.

"Well, in front of you is a wonderful tool that, if you learn to master it, will completely change your life by removing challenging situations," smiled Fiona.

Laura looked down at the piece of paper in front of her which read:

LESSON 6: Get a LIFE

Think of an action that you do for someone that you would like to stop doing or a request that you would like to say 'No' to but just can't seem to get the confidence to say it.

Write the situation, or request, down and use the following tool to regain your boundaries and transform your results.

L - Listen to the request made and repeat what you heard to the person asking.

I - Inform them of your situation.

F - Facts and figures should be used – avoid using emotions in this situation.

E - Elaborate on solutions available.

Noticing Laura looked a little confused, Fiona said "Let me talk you through a personal example of how I used this tool."

Fiona told the story of how once she had pencilled in a Friday afternoon for some quality time with her toddler but her demanding (and very important) client had no appreciation for Fiona's time and used to call her all hours of the day and night.

Frequently she would leave her toddler in front of the TV whilst she spent at least an hour or so on a call with the demanding client.

As you can imagine, Fiona got fed up with this. She felt torn between her VIP client (whose fees covered her mortgage and bills) and the most important person in her life – her toddler.

She didn't know how to fix it, so her body became physically ill in protest.

It was only when she became very ill that she used the 'Get a LIFE' lesson to say NO to her important client without having to actually saying NO.

"Here's what I did," she continued.

"I decided that I would treat my toddler like a VIP client. I would never leave a VIP client in a meeting room to fend for themselves for an hour or so whilst I jumped to the demands of another client who wanted to speak to me.

"Obviously I was deeply concerned that if I didn't jump when the client called, they may dump me. This client paid well and made up a huge chunk of my revenue.

"I had to approach this carefully.

"I considered what this client actually wanted and wrote out a plan of how I could deliver what was required for the client and also remain true to my boundaries of spending quality time with my no 1 VIP client – my toddler.

"Here's how my conversation with the client went:

[LISTEN]
I held a strategy day last week with my team and we analysed what our clients really need from us. After carefully considering your needs I believe you need 'XYZ'. It appears that you really value ad hoc and spontaneous access to our team for support with your urgent and important projects.

[INFORM]
As we've been working together from the outset, I can appreciate that you value our calls. Our company is growing and, as you can appreciate, I need to be there to help other clients through the early stages of setting up their accounts with us. I am torn between offering them an exceptional service and being 100% accountable to your account.

[FACTS & FIGURES]
I've worked through your accounts and reviewed all our calls and devised a plan of how I believe our company can best support you and your business in the most professional and cost-effective way.

[ELABORATE]
It is clear that you need skills and support in the following areas (XYZ). I have allocated three of our top specialists to support you in these areas. I will oversee your project and I propose that we have either a half day video conference call or a one to one meeting once every two weeks to review your full requirements. Of course, our top three executives assigned to your account will contact me immediately if they need my support but I can assure you they really are specialists in their field and really will add another dimension to your project. When are you free to meet the team?"

"Wow that really is a powerful tool!" exclaimed Laura. "I can see how this could be invaluable in transforming unreasonable demands on my time."

"I know, right?" joined in Fiona. "The great thing about this tool is the result – It's a win win result for all involved."

Laura nodded in agreement.

Fiona took a pad and pen out of her bag and handed it to Laura.

"What's this for?" Laura enquired.

"The fairies would go mad with me if I didn't insist that you go ahead now and write down some examples of how you are going to apply this tool when you return back to real life. said Fiona. "Off you go Laura, start writing!"

Laura took the pad and pen and instantly started writing.

When she crossed the last 't' and dotted the last 'i', the fairies appeared.

Despite being used to their spontaneous arrival, it still startled her.

Laura looked up and had to laugh at loud… Flo was wearing blue eye shadow and bright red lipstick.

"I'm sorry," apologised Laura. "You look very glamorous Flo, are you going somewhere nice?" enquired Laura, smiling at Hope and Fiona.

"She's trying to fit in," replied Hope on Flo's behalf. "I explained that we are fairies and invisible to most people but because we were going to a bar she wanted to make an extra effort," laughed Hope.

"It's been a long time since I've been on a girlie night out, especially in a bar" retorted Flo.

"In my day pubs were for men, and women stayed at home unless it was a special occasion – even then, men and women would drink in separate bars, not like these modern times with men and women all mix together in one room together. Times have changed and not for the better I might add!"

Hope, Fiona, and Laura giggled as they watched Flo lick salt from her hand, drink a shot of Tequila, and squirt lemon in her mouth.

"Right, that's enough for you" announced Hope escorting Flo away from the bar.

"Fiona, thank you so much for sharing Lesson 6 with Laura. Looking at what she's written, it seems like she's going to get huge value from the 'Get a LIFE' tool," beamed Hope and bent over to give Fiona a hug.

Fiona embraced Hope. "As always, it's my absolute pleasure. I mean that"

She turned to Laura, "I'd say 'Good Luck' but you and I both know that luck is not involved when transforming your life. It's mindset, belief, and action – and it seems to me that you have the right mix of all three so that you can get exactly what you want from your new life."

"Thanks Fiona. I trust that someday I will be, or even just look, as together as you do and am in a position to teach others the invaluable lesson you just taught me" Laura smiled.

"Ritch thennn," slurred Flo and hiccupped. "Let's get otta err"

It was Hope's turn to tut. She smiled fondly at Flo, pulled Laura to her, and waved goodbye to Fiona. Then with a blink of an eye they were off again.

SUMMARY OF LESSON 6

1. Be conscious of your boundaries and be clear on what you are 'giving up' by 'giving in' to demands that do not support your perfect life goal.

2. It is important to have boundaries and to positively let other people know they exist.

3. Aim to understand why people are benefitting from asking you to do things for them. It's important to see things from the perspective of others in order to create a win win solution for all.

4. Saying No without offering alternative solutions can ruin relationships. You will gain respect if you offer alternative helpful solutions to solve the challenges of others.

*****

I HAVE SEEN THE ENEMY AND IT IS… ME!

This time was different. Laura was standing outside her own house.

"Yesss! I'm home," she exclaimed with delight reaching to give Hope and Flo a big kiss.

"Sorry Laura, not yet. Look inside…" said Hope and gestured towards the lounge window.

Laura was transported back in time to a week ago, just before her conference.

The fairies told her to keep out of sight – the old self must never see the future self.

Laura peeked through the window and observed herself poring over a long To Do list, ticking them off as she threw items into a small suitcase.

She watched as her youngest child came in and asked if she could help. The old Laura batted her off with a swift, sharp tone "No sweetie, it's quicker if I do it myself."

The next scene appeared just as quickly as the last scene disappeared. This time she was dashing out the door to the supermarket to do the weekly shop. Her husband was repeatedly begging her to let him go instead but Laura once again batted the help aside, replying: "No I'll do it, I know where everything is, it'll be quicker," before dashing out the door slamming it behind her.

Before the scene disappeared she observed her husband shaking his head mumbling to himself. "Crazy… She doesn't even trust me to do a simple shopping trip. I'm not am imbecile. No wonder she's so stressed."

Laura gasped and put her hand to her mouth. A tear trickled down her cheek.

The fairies continued to replay scene after scene of Laura batting help aside. The fairies honed in on the sadness and disappointment shown on the faces of those whose offers of help had been shunned.

At last, the scenes blurred then vanished.

Laura and the fairies were once again alone. Laura stood shaking and crying. "That was very cruel of you," she blurted out in between sobs.

"Stupid me. All this time I thought I had to do everything myself but my family, friends and colleagues were trying to help and support me – I just wouldn't let them and everyone suffered. I made them feel inadequate, incompetent, redundant. And most importantly, I didn't make time for them."

Tears continued to flow. Flo tutted and handed her a clean hankie. "Now that's enough dear. What's done is done. The question now is, 'What are you going to do differently when you return to normal life?'"

"Normal life? Ha!" laughed Laura. "If that's normal life I don't ever want to return to it again. How am I ever going to look my family and friends in the eye knowing how badly I've treated them?"

Hope stepped in. "We've only shown you this lesson Laura to help you. No one will remember being hurt. They love you and they will still offer to help because they want the best for you. You wanted to change, you wanted a better life. We have shown you how you have behaved so you can take lessons learnt and apply them to create a better future for yourself.

"No one is judging you. You are not alone. We continuously notice women that look like they're under control but most women aren't. They spend so much of their time pretending to have it all together but they're like swans – underneath that calm façade, they're paddling like hell below the water just trying to keep afloat. They're all doing their best to make it through a busy day – a stressful day often caused by their own doing.

"Imagine if we got all the working mums of the world together and asked them to be open and honest with each other. Imagine if they stopped and admitted that they have taken on too much and really needed some help. The whole nation would breathe a sigh of relief and I bet you everyone would turn around and start offering assistance. Then imagine further, if you can, everyone turning around and accepting the assistance offered."

Laura smiled as she imagined how her life would change if she asked – and accepted – help.

"In my day we didn't ask for help. We had a good stiff upper lip, our men were busy working and we were busy doing household chores and bringing up children, looking after elderly parents and 50 other things that you lot have machines for these days," Flo interjected crossly.

"And that's exactly why these poor working mums are struggling today, Flo!" Hope said firmly. "They were set that example but now they are trying to work and take full responsibility for the home too. Times have changed, Flo. Women need to learn to embrace that and acknowledge that if they want to have it all they have to share the workload and ask for help – it's as simple as that."

Flo looked offended and muttered under her breath "Hmph, seems that looking after the house isn't enough for women these days – poor men having to work and then come home and cook dinner too. Women want to be able to have their cake and eat it these days!"

Hope and Laura looked at each other and laughed.

"Allow me to respond Laura," said Hope before turning to her colleague. "Both men and women can have their cake and eat it these days, Flo, and it's a much better party to be at now especially if everyone gets stuck into the baking and party preparations"

"Amen to that," grinned Laura.

LESSON 7: Delegate & Say 'Yes' To Offers Of Help

Hope handed Laura a pen and paper and asked her to complete the following activity:

- Review Lesson 5's actions to delegate.
- Review Lesson 4's Milestone Magic goals.
- Next to each item write who can assist with the activity/action.

'You wrote the right things, Laura, but your facial expression and body language are giving off a very different message?" questioned Hope.

"I know," replied Laura. "I'm so transparent," she giggled. "As the saying goes 'I have seen the enemy and it is me! I now recognise myself as a control freak and I'm uncomfortable handing over my tasks to other people. But, as you said at the beginning, 'If I want to make a positive change in my life and improve my family life I have to start letting go."

"Praise the lord!" declared Flo, laughing and raising her hands.

"That was a very powerful lesson," Laura continued. "Being a martyr doesn't bring an enjoyable easy life. I can't wait to start accepting and asking for help. I'm going to have so much time on my hands!"

"Good for you," replied Hope. "Now your past self is about to come out the back door and we can't let her see you so we need to dash. Let me help you over the garden fence…"

"It's okay, I can do it," huffed Laura as she tried to scramble over the high fence.

"Really?" Hope exclaimed "After all we just taught you?"

Laura rolled her eyes at herself "What I actually meant to say was 'Yes please, Hope, I would love some help.' Please give me a leg up!"

"I can do better than that," offered Flo. She waved her wand and in a flash, they were off on another adventure.

SUMMARY OF LESSON 7

1. Learn how to let go of being a perfectionist.

2. Be conscious of people offering help.

3. Be gracious and accept help.

4. Get great at saying "Thank you!"

*****

FILL YOUR OWN CUP

Laura opened her eyes and found herself in a swimsuit, wrapped in big, fluffy white robe.

Taking in her surrounding, Laura saw that she was in a spa. She whooped with delight!

To her left was an outdoor hot tub and a Zen garden to her right. Directly in front of her was a room with a sign above the door that read 'Greek Herbal Experience – step inside and enjoy the relaxing fragrance of sage, chamomile and rosemary'.

Laura could hardly believe her eyes. She loved spas but never had the time to go. Well that's not entirely true – she could make the time but because she worked full-time hours she always felt guilty about leaving the children for a day or even an afternoon.

Laura recognised that this guilt wasn't restricted to spas, she also felt guilty doing anything for her own personal enjoyment.

"Penny for your thoughts?" interrupted Hope.

"Nothing really, I have mixed feelings about spas. I love them but feel guilty enjoying things when I should be at home looking after my children."

"Quite right" said Flo, sounding a little out of breath. Laura stifled a giggle when she turned to see a perspiring Flo fully dressed in outdoor clothing, wearing a dressing gown.

"What on earth are you wearing, Flo?" Hope exclaimed

"I'm not exposing my body – it's indecent," blurted out Flo. "Anyway, you're right to feel guilty Laura. In my day a mother's place was in the home and you never went out unless it was a special occasion and only then on your husband's arm."

Hope looked at an open mouthed Laura. "Don't even respond, Laura"

"You're not alone with that feeling, Laura. The majority of mothers, working or not, feel guilty at spending 'time out' away from their children. That's why I'm going to introduce you to a very special woman whose story will help you appreciate that 'time out' is essential for the good health of any mum – physical and emotional."

Hope opened the door to the Greek Herbal Room and gestured Laura to step in then closed the door gently behind her.

Inside was dimly lit and steam swirled gently around the marble seats. The whole room was decorated in blue and purple mosaics and in the middle of the room housed a wooden device nesting the herbs; sage, chamomile and rosemary. The smell was divine and the steam soothing. The room was so inviting that Laura couldn't help but breath in the fragrance, settle relaxingly into a seat close her eyes and then let out a huge sigh: "Ahhhhhh!"

"Wow, that's a big sigh for one so petite." A voice rang out of the darkness.

Laura was jolted back into her body, opened her eyes and saw a smiling women in her mid thirties, looking at her.

"Hi Laura, I've been expecting you. I'm Jo and I have so much to tell you so would you mind if we brush past pleasantries and get straight into Lesson 8?"

"Go ahead," replied Laura. "I know I'm going to enjoy this lesson, please teach me everything you know, Jo…" Laura breathed in the aroma, closed her eyes, exhaled slowly and instantly began to relax.

"I'm an air hostess, working exclusively on long haul flights. I love my job and get to see some wonderful countries but, although the overnight stays are always in beautiful, luxury hotels, I never enjoy them because I felt I should really be at home with my children.

"I'd look out of my hotel room at the wonderful city views and chastise myself for not being home to see the best view of all – my children sleeping!

"I felt guilty when working and when I returned I would spend every waking moment with the children to overcome this feeling of guilt. I didn't see friends or even go out with my husband because that would take me away from the children.

"In the end my husband left me for another woman who gave him some attention, my children became demanding of me and my time and suffered with anxiety attacks when I left them to go to work. My friends stopped asking me out.

"Even though I sometimes went out with the people at work and spent time with the children at home I felt lonely. Eventually I became resentful which presented itself as one illness after another.

"It was when I was lying in bed feeling sorry for myself that Hope and Flo appeared. They told me that people teach what they most need to learn.
As you can imagine I was confused and was concerned for my mental state of mind but they continued.

"They said before the airplane leaves the tarmac I always run through some safety instructions including this one: 'In the unlikely event that cabin pressure changes, oxygen mask will automatically drop. Pull the mask towards you and place it over your nose and mouth. Strap it over your head and tighten it. Breathe normally. It is normal that the oxygen bag will not fully inflate. Please ensure to adjust your own mask before assisting others'

"They asked me why do I advise people, especially mothers, to put on their own mask before assisting others, their children. I explained that if a mother is not safe and well she is no use to her children and everyone will then be put in danger. The fairies remained silent as they let me take in the words I had just announced – the sentence hung over me like a heavy cloud yet I felt completely enlightened.

"I realised that my job allowed me to create a safe home for me and my family. When I was at work their father, grandparents, and my very close friends looked after my children so they felt incredibly cared for, safe and loved.

"I wasn't depriving them while working abroad – it wasn't ideal but it left me free to spend good quality time with them on the days I was at home and at weekends.

"I provided for them financially and emotionally and bestowed all my love upon them but I then recognized that if I didn't enjoy my own life, 'put on my own mask' so to speak, I would be no use to anyone.

"It's no wonder my husband and I separated. If I didn't care about and respect myself, why should anyone else?

"The fairies made me realise that no one would lose out if I enjoyed myself whilst away from home. In fact, I would come back feeling alive and uplifted. I would have stories to tell and be full of fun and laughter.

"Also, by showing my children that I enjoyed myself at work, as well as enjoying my time at home with them, I would be empowering them to do the same when they become parents too.

"After that magical insightful moment I realised that my family are top priority and always will be but that doesn't mean I should ignore my own needs, I matter too.

"Since then I enjoy my time out when I travel with work, I also have girlie weekend breaks, the odd night out, and coffee with friends whenever I can.

"I started taking time out once a month to have a spa session. I still can't make the mental leap to taking a full day out but I'm learning.

"Actually, the funny thing is, whilst I'm here the children are at a party. The old me would just be at home now cleaning up but instead I'm here filling my own cup. I'll pick them up in a few hours feeling re-energised and looking fabulous 'darlink!"

"Good for you!" said Laura who was now sitting at the edge of her seat hanging onto Jo's every word. "I am so inspired by your story. I can totally relate to everything you said and can see that I too have been failing to put on my own mask."

"Let's settle down in the relaxation lounge so you can write down what you have learnt from Lesson 8," suggested Jo.

A moment later the ladies were cocooned in the relaxation area. Tranquil music played in the background and therapists approached with Chinese teapots containing refreshing herbal tea.

LESSON 8: Look After Yourself Before Others

Laura took a sip and Jo handed her a pad and pen.

"Over to you now Laura… what action are you going to take when you get back to ensure you not only fill your own cup but ensure it overfloweth…?" laughed Jo.

Laura took the pen and started making a long list. When she finished she reviewed the list and looked up at Jo. "Well, that felt very self-indulgent…"

"That's the whole point of Lesson 8. You'd better get used to self-indulging because I can guarantee that once you fill your own cup others will automatically benefit from your uplifted spirit," declared Jo.

"I'm going to take a moment now to do something I love... I'm going to write down Lesson 8 so I always remember this one," laughed Laura.

Laura finished the list and closed her eyes, took a deep breath through her nose and exhaled slowly through her mouth.

She felt relaxed, calm, and so very grateful for the gift of time and self-reflection bestowed on her by the fairies.

"Ahhh you both look very serene," announced Hope appearing out of thin air.

"Ohhh we are," said Jo and Laura in unison.

"Lesson 8 is my absolute favourite lesson," exclaimed Laura with delight.

"Yes, it's a contented mum's best kept secret," shared Hope.

"Psst, can we get out of here now," whispered Flo in a harried voice. "I'm sweltering in this dressing gown," she added.

Jo and Laura laughed as they turned to see Flo peering from behind a pillar mopping sweat from her face with a hankie since she was still fully dressed and wearing a white robe and had added socks and flip flops to her spa outfit.

Hope hid a smirk and shook her head.

"Come on Laura, let's get Flo out of here before she passes out or gets arrested. Thank you, Jo, for sharing Lesson 8. Send our love to your family when you meet up with them later today and keep up the great work of filling your own cup - you look positively radiant!"

Jo blushed, smiled, and sat back to enjoy some more moments of tranquility just as Laura and the fairies disappeared in a puff of steam.

SUMMARY OF LESSON 8

1. Remember that others benefit when you feel happy and relaxed.

2. Make a list of what makes you feel great.

3. Ring fence and honour time to enjoy doing things you love.

4. Let go of guilt as it doesn't serve you.

5. Encourage others to do things that make them feel great.

*****

PSST ... I HAVE A SECRET

Laura opened her eyes and found herself back in her kitchen. She checked the date and time on her iPad and shrieked with pleasure "Yes! I'm home", she exclaimed with delight. "I'm going to wake the family up and tell them all about my adventures, they won't believe it I'm sure" she added.

"Whoa there Laura, you're right... they won't believe it and it's still a little too early to wake them up," suggested Hope. "Let's take a few moments to reflect together on your 'Adventure' and for you to share with us what you've learnt."

"Sure. What's a few moments when you have a whole wonderful life ahead of you," responded Laura almost too enthusiastically.

Flo arrived with a freshly squeezed orange juice and placed it in front of Laura. "Okay Working Mum... I know I have learnt a lesson or two but go ahead what have you learnt this evening?"

"Welllll Flo..." replied Laura sternly. "I have learnt that I need to define what I want and not give focus to what I don't want. Once I have defined what I want I need to create MAGIC goals which are very clear and explicit about what I want.

"Next I need to understand what has stopped me from getting what I want so far, my obstacles, and then work out solutions to overcome these obstacles should I face them again in the future.

"I also need to appreciate that my Magic goals could be too overwhelming so I need to chunk them down into smaller milestone MAGIC goals so I remain motivated and inspired to take action.

"Talking of action I should only focus on five to nine actions – at any one time, as our brains can only focus on five to nine items at any one time, and I don't need a Plan B as it detracts from Plan A.

"I can't keep doing the same thing over and over again expecting a different result so I have to identify what I am doing that adds or detracts from my MAGIC goals. If the actions I take each day do not add value I should stop doing them or delegate them.

"I need to understand that if it is hard to achieve my MAGIC goals I should just ask the question 'Do I want it enough?' and wonder whether my old beliefs, or ways of doing things, are getting in the way of my growth. If I am doing things that don't contribute to my MAGIC goals I should introduce my newly discovered tool 'Get a LIFE' which will transform the situation into a win win result.

"I'm going to learn how to let go of my limiting belief that I have to do everything myself in order for it to be perfect. Good enough is good enough. When people offer help I am going to be gracious enough to accept it.

"I am going to be unashamedly self-indulgent because now I know that if I am happy I have more energy and I can share that positive energy with those I love so we all benefit.

"I think that's it, yes it is," summarised Laura.

"By jove I think she's got it," said Flo to Hope in a cockney accent imitating a My Fair Lady moment.

"We're sooo proud," said Flo and Hope, standing together with their hands crossed over their hearts and beaming like proud parents.

"Ahhh you guys - bring it in," cheered Laura opening her arms and welcoming the fairies in for a group hug.

"Okay our work here is almost done," added Flo. "We just have to leave you with a little rule list and a disclaimer," she said, handing over two sheets of paper and a pen to Laura.

ABIDE BY THESE RULES FOLLOWING A VISIT FROM A FAIRY/FAIRIES

1. Follow the 8 lessons learnt and take action everyday towards your MAGIC goals
2. If you lose motivation revisit the lessons learnt
3. Approach life positively and avoid negative words and thoughts
4. Be conscious of all the good in your life and give thanks for it
5. Approach life with an abundant mind set rather than one of lack
6. Follow the rule of karma, give without expectation and you shall receive
7. Share the lessons learnt with other working mums
8. Never judge or compare yourself to other mothers – we are all just doing our best.
9. You really can have it all.
10. You only have one life so enjoy it!

When Laura had finished reading the rules, she found that she was smiling. She then turned her attention to the Declaration which read:

DECLARATION FOLLOW A VISIT FROM THE FAIRIES

After a visit from the fairies thou shalt share lessons learnt and abide by the rules but thou shalt not speak of the event directly on account that no one will believe you and if they did the fairy underground world may be uncovered thus causing all fairies to live in hot robes with socks and flip flops for the rest of their lives.

I ………………………. [your name] swear I will abide by the declaration rules.

Laura took the pen and signed her name. "Did you write the declaration, Flo?" questioned Laura, chuckling to herself.

"How ever did you guess?" wondered Flo.

"Just a wild guess inspired by a little spa incident" Laura replied, catching a wink and a stifled laugh from Hope.

"Okay, Laura, this is it ... Now's the time to ride your bike without stabilisers ... Are you ready?" questioned Hope.

"Absolutely!" Exclaimed Laura with delight.

"Okay in your words 'Bring it in' and let's hug this happy ending out," said Hope opened armed.

Flo and Laura embraced Hope and the fairies disappeared.

'Ohh I wasn't expecting that,' said Laura to herself.

She noticed how sad she felt that the fairies were no longer around and she also had a slight sense of desperation and anxiety that she was now alone in her kitchen where she started this journey potentially in a place where nothing had changed.

What if she didn't remember the rules? What if she didn't have the strength to follow them or have the courage to see the MAGIC goals through?

Just then she heard a knock at the door. She looked at her watch, it was 7am. Who could be knocking at this early hour?

Laura shook herself out of her daze and opened the door to find a parcel, beautifully wrapped, in sparkling paper on the door step.

She looked left and right but the deliverer was nowhere to be seen. Laura lifted the pretty parcel off the step, closed the door behind her, and made her way to the kitchen counter.

She opened the parcel. Inside was a note from her boss, it read:

Dear Laura,

You may have thought that I have taken you for granted recently but via this small gesture I wanted you to know that your hard work and dedication to the company has not gone unnoticed.

We won a really big client during the event you just organised and attended. The client has asked to work with you exclusively. She is a working mum who values a work life balance. She likes to play hard and work hard and she felt that you had the same values.

In celebration of this win, and in acknowledgement that you have had little time with your family lately, we have cleared your diary for today and look forward to welcoming you back into the office for a meeting with your new client tomorrow.

Please enjoy the contents of the box.

Harry

"Yes!" shouted Laura with delight.

She lifted the next layer of paper wrapping to review the contents of the box. Inside were the following:

- Tickets to the cinema for an early PM show.
- Dinner reservations for her children's family favourite restaurant - all expenses paid.
- A DVD - In Pursuit of Happiness.
- A book entitled "Working Mum, Mission Impossible?

Laura picked up the book and flicked through the index. The book slipped out of her hands and opened to expose the inside front cover, it read:

To the reader,

We trust the contents of this book will change your life for the better. Read, digest, and enjoy putting it into action.

Your believing eyes.

Hope and Flo.

Laura had a smile that reached from ear to ear.

Just then the dog's tail started wagging frantically as her two beautiful daughters ran through the kitchen door shouting "Mummy, Mummy, you're home... We missed you so much."

Pete followed closely behind yawning like a big papa bear and kissed her on the head as he made his way to the coffee machine.

Amy and Jemma perched on the breakfast counter and shouted in unison: "What's for breakfast?"

Laura looked in the cupboard and fridge and replied, "How about pancakes?"

"Yippee!" squealed Amy and Jemma, again in unison.

"And why don't we make lots of them so we can turn them into a pancake cake for school cake bake?" Suggested Laura.

"Really?" questioned Amy. "Is that allowed?"

"Anything is allowed as long as it is baked with love. If it just happens to taste great too well that's just an added bonus," replied Laura, winking at Amy.

"You all relax and wake up and I will start making them..." Laura started, then looked at her family's faces showing disappointment.

"Or... you can show me how to make the best pancakes in town whilst I put my feel up and take on the task of chief taster?"

"I'll get the pans," said Pete

"I'll mix the pancake batter," said Jemma

"I am in charge of the decoration as it's my cake," added Amy bossily.

Laura watched on feeling happy and content. What a difference a night makes, she thought to herself.

Hope and Flo were watching through the window.

"Another happy ending fairytale," chuckled Flo

"Indeed," replied Hope. "Looks like our work here is done Flo. I just trust that Laura will keep the book to hand and following it because, if she does, she will know that all things are possible"

"Did you give her my book too?," asked Flo.

"Ohhh nooo... Sorry Flo I completely forgot to put it in the box," replied Hope reaching for the book in her fairy sack.

"Sorry Flo, here it is. Why don 't you keep it safe for our next working mum she may need it more?" said Hope, popping her arm around Flo's shoulder and handing her a book titled 'You can't have your cake and eat it'.

"I much prefer that title to your original one, Flo"

"Really? I much prefer, 'In my day mothers stayed at home'," Flo huffed, and grabbed the book.

"Ohh I do love you Flo," said Hope.

"In the words of Patrick Swayze, ditto," growled Flo, grabbing the manuscript and whisking her off in a puff of smoke.

*****

HAVE YOU BEEN INSPIRED?

There is nothing more powerful than hearing success, or lessons learnt, stories from other working mums. If you have something to share, big or small, please visit **www.leanneflower.co.uk** for details on submitting your stories.

LEANNE FLOWER

Leanne Flower has over 25 years' proven experience in Learning & Development and Human Resources. She is a qualified life, career, and business/executive coach, TAP accredited trainer, Joint Education Board qualified and experienced lecturer, and a CIPD member.

Leanne is also qualified in Reiki and Crystal Healing and uses these mindfulness techniques to reduce stress and empower her clients.

As a working mother of twin girls, Leanne walks her talk and welcomes opportunities to share tools and techniques regarding managing work, homelife, and how to successfully juggle multiple jobs/contracts.

She has a wealth of client testimonials on LinkedIn and happily shares client success stories on her website www.leanneflower.co.uk

She is available on request to train, coach, and speak to inspire and motivate working mums across the globe.

Contact **leanne@leanneflower.co.uk or visit www.leanneflower.co.uk**

WORK WITH ME

One to One Life Coaching:
Great if you are stuck in a rut, at a cross-roads, need someone to talk to in a safe and confidential environment, need some help getting motivated to take action or to make change, or just want some help deciding what you do want.

Career Coaching:
Perfect if you have been made redundant; Looking to secure a promotion; Fancy getting back into work after a career break; Want to change vocation; Or just need some help finding out what career will make you happy.

Coaching Programmes:
If you enjoy working in a group, or want to sign up to a longer-term support structure, then you may be interested in learning about our Coaching Programmes. There is a variety to choose from which run at different times of the year. Visit www.leanneflower.co.uk/coaching/coaching-programmes

Workshops & Retreats:

Each workshop or retreat is jam packed full of content and come with the promise of providing you with great insight to change your life for the better.

Training courses:
Choose from bespoke or off the shelf leadership & management and/or wellbeing & mindfulness courses

Motivational Speaker:
Book me for your event for an engaging, thought provoking, talk or presentation perfectly designed to inspire and motivate your audience.

Visit **www.leanneflower.co.uk** to learn more or email Leanne@leanneflower.co.uk

Printed in Great Britain
by Amazon